easy cakes

RYLAND
PETERS
& SMALL
LONDON NEW YORK

easy cakes

Linda Collister

photography by Diana Miller

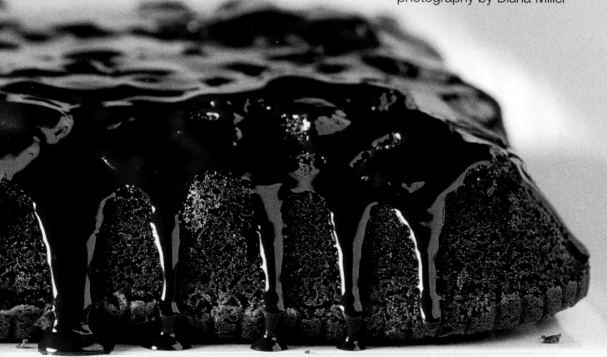

First published in the United States
in 2004
by Ryland Peters & Small, Inc.
519 Broadway, 5th Floor
New York, NY 10012
www.rylandpeters.com

10 9 8 7 6 5 4 3 2 1

Library of Congress
Cataloging-in-Publication Data

Collister, Linda.
  Easy cakes / Linda Collister ;
photography by Diana Miller.
    p. cm.
  ISBN 1-84172-713-X
  1. Cake. 2. Cookery, American.
I. Title.
  TX771.C56 2004
  641.8'653--dc22
          2004003811

Dedication
To my lovely in-laws.

Acknowledgments
I would to thank the many people who
helped with this book; Elsa Petersen-
Schepelern, Steve Painter, Susan Stuck,
Diana Miller, Bridget Sargeson, Vicky
Keppel-Compton, Róisín Nield, Barbara
Levy, Simon Silverwood, Shelley Rau,
Annette and Will Hertz, Alan Hertz,
Robert Carmack, and Michelle Kershaw.

Senior Designer Steve Painter
Commissioning Editor
    Elsa Petersen-Schepelern
Editor Susan Stuck
Production Patricia Harrington
Art Director Gabriella Le Grazie
Publishing Director Alison Starling

Food Stylist Bridget Sargeson
Stylist Róisín Nield

Notes
• All spoon measurements are level
unless otherwise specified.
• All eggs are extra-large unless
otherwise specified. Uncooked or
partially cooked eggs should not be
served to the very young, the very old,
those with compromised immune
systems, or to pregnant women.
• Before baking, weigh or measure all
ingredients exactly and prepare baking
pans and other utensils.
• Ovens should be preheated to the
specified temperature. Recipes in this
book were tested in several kinds of
oven—all work slightly differently.
I recommend using an oven thermometer
and consulting the manufacturer's
handbook for special instructions.

contents

6   a piece of cake ...

8   layer cakes

18   bundt cakes

40   daisy cakes

52   other cakes

60   toppings and sauces

64   index and conversion chart

a piece of cake ...

"A piece of cake" is something simple, and here is a collection of pieces of cake: easy to make, great to look at, delicious to eat.

The keys to good cake baking are not complex recipes or great skill; the keys are practice, care, and good, fresh ingredients. Unless you have a patisserie or a farmers' market on your doorstep, no cake you buy will be as delicious as one you bake yourself. Fresh, free-range eggs, real unsalted butter, true vanilla, good chocolate, fresh nuts and spices, and quality dried fruit give flavor that can't be beaten.

How can you make baking easy? First, get to know your equipment. Turn on the oven well in advance so it is thoroughly heated and ready for the cake; some ovens take 15 minutes to reach the correct temperature. Also, ovens vary and thermostats can be unreliable, so check the temperature with an oven thermometer. Some convexion ovens also recommend a slightly lower oven temperature.

An electric mixer is invaluable for beating and mixing; it will save you a lot of time and energy. For effective mixing, ingredients should be at room temperature, unless the recipe says otherwise. Don't forget to scrape down the bowl from time to time.

When you buy cake pans, read the maker's notes carefully—some pans have coatings which require special treatment. Because they will bake faster, they should be used at a lower temperature or for less time. Look out for good-quality pans with nonstick coatings, and use pre-cut or readymade paper liners. If you brush inside the pan with melted unsalted butter, unmolding the cake after baking will be no problem.

Home baking was a great European tradition, and cakes are still an important part of it. They include delicate, airy cakes of France and Italy; sweet, enriched, fruit-flecked bread doughs from Germany and the heart of Europe; rich spice cakes from Scandinavia; hearty fruitcakes from Britain and Ireland. Each wave of immigrants to North America brought along their favorite recipes and ingredients as well as cooking pans. The Bundt pan, now the quintessential American cake pan, started out in Central Europe a couple hundred years ago when bakers put a metal tube in the center of their large, deep, cake molds to help the middle bake more evenly and let it rise higher. These developed into the elaborate kugelhopf molds still used in Alsace, and the huge range and fancy, detailed designs of heavy, metal Bundt pans.

Finally, a word about coffee cakes. Until I married an American, I thought these were regular cakes flavored with real coffee. Now I know this ain't necessarily so. For my husband, coffee cake is a cake accompanied by a cup of coffee at any time of the day—breakfast, mid-morning, mid-afternoon—or as a dessert. This tradition comes from Germany and Central Europe. There, even the simplest meal was concluded with, or consisted of, coffee and a sweet bake. What civilized people!

layer cakes

If you can make muffins, you can make this cake. It is really a rich chocolate chip muffin recipe, so just measure and mix. The frosting is a simple butter mixture made with cocoa.

triple chocolate layer cake

3 cups self-rising flour

⅔ cup unsweetened cocoa powder

a good pinch of salt

2 cups sugar

1 cup sunflower oil

2 extra-large eggs, beaten

1 cup milk

1 teaspoon pure vanilla extract

1 cup semi-sweet chocolate chips, plus extra to decorate

frosting

1 stick plus 1 tablespoon unsalted butter, at room temperature

2¾ cups confectioners' sugar, sifted

6 tablespoons unsweetened cocoa powder, sifted

¼ cup milk

½ teaspoon pure vanilla extract

3 cake pans, 8 inches diameter, greased and bottoms lined with parchment paper

makes one 3-layer cake

To make the cake, sift the flour, cocoa, salt, and sugar into a large bowl, and make a hollow in the center. Pour the oil, beaten eggs, milk, and vanilla into the hollow in the dry ingredients, and mix gradually with a wooden spoon. Add the chocolate chips and stir well. Divide the mixture between the 3 prepared pans.

Bake in a preheated oven at 350°F for 20–25 minutes or until a skewer inserted in the center comes out clean. Let the cakes cool in the pans for 5 minutes, then carefully invert onto a wire rack and let cool completely.

Meanwhile, to make the frosting, put the soft butter in a bowl and, using a wooden spoon or an electric mixer, beat until very creamy. Gradually beat in the confectioners' sugar, cocoa, milk, and vanilla to make a thick, smooth frosting.

When the cakes are completely cold, use the frosting to layer them. Spread about one-sixth of the frosting on the top of one cake. Gently set a second cake on top and spread with another one-sixth of the frosting. Top with the last cake, then coat the top and sides with the rest of the frosting. Decorate with extra chocolate chips.

Store in an airtight container and eat within 4 days.

An elegant, mile-high, three-layer cake, feather-light but full of rich flavors. The maple syrup frosting can be replaced with whipped cream flavored with maple sugar—Maple Cream (page 61).

maple syrup pecan cake

3 sticks unsalted butter, at room temperature

1⅓ cups sugar

4 extra-large eggs, lightly beaten

3 tablespoons pure maple syrup

1¼ cup pecan pieces, finely chopped (in a food processor), but not ground

2⅓ cups self-rising flour, sifted

a pinch of salt

frosting

1 cup pure maple syrup

2 extra-large egg whites

pecan halves, to decorate

a rubber spatula

3 cake pans, 8 inches diameter, greased and the bottoms lined with parchment paper

makes one 3-layer cake

Using an electric mixer, beat the butter until lighter in color, then add the sugar, a spoonful at a time, while still beating. When all the sugar has been added, scrape down the sides of the bowl, then beat until the mixture is very light and fluffy. Beat in the eggs a spoonful at a time, then gradually beat in the maple syrup. Add the pecans, flour, and salt and, using a large metal spoon or rubber spatula, gently fold into the mixture.

Divide the mixture between the 3 prepared pans and spread evenly. Bake in a preheated oven at 350°F for 25–30 minutes, until the cakes are golden and springy to the touch. Let cool for a minute, then run a round-bladed knife around the inside edge of the pans to loosen the cakes and carefully invert onto a wire rack to cool.

Meanwhile, to make the frosting, heat the maple syrup in a medium, heavy saucepan and let boil gently until it reaches 238°F on a candy thermometer (softball stage)—5 minutes if you don't have a thermometer. Take care, because the syrup can bubble up and boil over if the heat is too high. While the syrup is heating, beat the egg whites until stiff peaks form using an electric mixer or whisk. Pour the hot syrup onto the egg whites in a thin stream while still beating constantly. Keep beating for a further 1 minute or until the frosting is very thick and fluffy.

Use the frosting to layer the cakes. Spread about one-sixth of the frosting on the top of one cake. Gently set a second cake on top and spread with one-sixth of the frosting. Top with the last cake, then coat the top and sides with the rest of the frosting. Decorate with pecan halves.

This cake is very delicate—it cuts best the next day. Store at room temperature in an airtight container. Best eaten within 4 days.

A weird but wonderfully exotic recipe from Australia—a moist, fresh fruitcake packed with flavor. Use a small, fresh pineapple or a carton of ready-prepared fresh pineapple. Leave plain, or decorate with dried banana chips or candied pineapple chunks.

fresh pineapple layer cake

7 oz. trimmed fresh pineapple (scant 1 cup pulp)

6 oz. peeled ripe bananas (about 2 small)

1¾ cups self-rising flour

½ teaspoon baking powder

a good pinch of salt

½ teaspoon ground cinnamon

a good pinch of freshly grated nutmeg

1 cup firmly packed moist light brown sugar

2 extra-large eggs, beaten

1 cup safflower oil

frosting

6 oz. cream cheese (⅔ cup)

4 tablespoons unsalted butter, at room temperature

1 cup plus 2 tablespoons confectioners' sugar, sifted

1 tablespoon lemon juice

2 cake pans, 8 inches diameter, greased and bottoms lined with parchment paper

makes one 2-layer cake

Put the pineapple in a food processor and blend until fairly finely chopped, or chop with a knife, saving all the juice. Mash the bananas coarsely with a fork.

Sift the flour, baking powder, salt, cinnamon, and nutmeg into a large bowl. Mix in the brown sugar, then make a hollow in the center. Put the prepared pineapple and bananas, eggs, and oil in the hollow, then mix all the ingredients together with a wooden spoon. When thoroughly mixed, divide between the 2 prepared pans, and spread evenly.

Bake in a preheated oven at 350°F for 30–35 minutes until firm to the touch. Leave for a minute, then run a knife around the inside of the pan to loosen the cakes. Invert onto a wire rack and let cool completely.

To make the frosting, beat the cream cheese and butter with an electric mixer or whisk. Using low speed, beat in the confectioners' sugar, 1 tablespoon at a time. Add lemon juice to taste.

Use the frosting to layer the cakes. Spread about one-half of the frosting on the top of one cake. Gently set the second cake on top, then coat the top and sides with the remaining frosting. Serve at room temperature.

Store in an airtight container in a cool pantry or refrigerator and eat within 4 days.

A simple vanilla cake filled with whipped cream, good vanilla fudge (homemade or from a speciality store), and sliced bananas. If you prefer a cake that doesn't need to be kept in the refrigerator, use the Toffee Topping (page 61). Real fudge fans can decorate the cake with small pieces of extra fudge.

banana-vanilla fudge cake

1½ sticks unsalted butter, softened

¾ cup sugar

2 tablespoons moist light brown sugar

3 extra-large eggs, at room temperature, beaten

2½ cups self-rising flour

½ teaspoon pure vanilla extract

1 tablespoon milk

filling and frosting

1¼ cups heavy cream, chilled

4½ oz. vanilla fudge, chilled

2 ripe medium bananas, thinly sliced

extra fudge, to decorate, (optional)

3 cake pans, 8 inches diameter, greased and bottoms lined with parchment paper

makes one 3-layer cake

To make the cake, put the butter, white and brown sugars, beaten eggs, flour, vanilla, and milk in a large bowl. Beat at medium speed with an electric mixer or whisk until smooth and thoroughly blended. Divide the mixture between the 3 prepared pans and spread evenly.

Bake in a preheated oven at 350°F for about 20 minutes, until just firm to the touch. Let cool for a minute, then run a round-bladed knife inside the rim of the pan just to loosen the cakes. Invert onto a wire rack and let cool completely.

When ready to assemble, put the cream in a chilled bowl and whip until soft peaks form. Grate the fudge onto the cream and gently stir in. Set one layer of cake on a serving platter, spread with a third of the cream, and cover with half the banana slices. Top with another layer of cake and spread with half the remaining cream, top with the rest of the bananas, then finally add the last layer of cake. Spread the remaining cream on top of the cake.

Keep cool and eat the same day, or store in an airtight container in the refrigerator and eat within 2 days.

A good cake for a party, this one looks wonderful and cuts easily. The vanilla cake is baked in a square pan, cut into two strips, then sandwiched with jam and topped with whipped cream and fresh berries.

raspberries-and-cream layer cake

2 sticks unsalted butter, softened

1 cup plus 2 tablespoons sugar

4 extra-large eggs, at room temperature, beaten

½ teaspoon pure vanilla extract

1 tablespoon milk

1¾ cups self-rising flour

½ teaspoon baking powder

filling and topping

5–6 tablespoons Fresh Raspberry (or strawberry) Preserve (page 62)

1 cup heavy cream, chilled

4 cups (1 lb.) small ripe berries, hulled

a nonstick square cake pan 9 x 9 x 2 inches, greased

makes one 2-layer cake

To make the cake, put the butter in a large bowl, then add the sugar, eggs, vanilla, milk, flour, and baking powder. Beat with an electric mixer or whisk using medium speed. When very smooth and thoroughly mixed, spoon the mixture into the prepared pan and spread evenly, right into the corners.

Bake in a preheated oven at 350°F for about 25 minutes, or until the cake just springs back when gently pressed in the center. Remove the pan from the oven and let cool for 10 minutes before inverting onto a wire rack.

Using a large, sharp knife or bread knife, trim off the edges, then cut the cake in half down its length to make 2 long strips.

Set 1 strip on a serving platter, then spread with the preserve. Top with the second layer of cake and press down gently. Whip the cream until very thick and soft peaks form, then spread over the top of the cake. Decorate with berries and serve.

Store in an airtight container in the refrigerator and eat within 3 days.

bundt cakes

Serve warm with Toffee Sauce (page 61) for a real treat.

The moist texture comes from the cold applesauce.

chocolate spice cake

1 cup all-purpose flour

½ cup unsweetened cocoa powder

½ teaspoon baking powder

1 teaspoon baking soda

a pinch of salt

1 teaspoon ground cinnamon

1 teaspoon ground ginger

1¼ cups firmly packed moist light brown sugar

¼ cup safflower oil

2 extra-large eggs, beaten

⅔ cup sour cream

⅓ cup unsweetened applesauce

3 tablespoons chopped crystallized ginger

confectioners' sugar, for dusting

Toffee Topping or Toffee Sauce (page 61), to serve

a cathedral or other Bundt pan, 9 inches diameter, well greased

makes one Bundt cake

Sift the flour, cocoa, baking powder, baking soda, salt, cinnamon, and ground ginger into a large bowl. Mix in the sugar and make a hollow in the center.

Put the oil, eggs, sour cream, and applesauce in another bowl and beat well. Add to the hollow in the dry ingredients and stir gently until thoroughly mixed. Stir in the crystallized ginger.

Pour into the prepared pan and bake in a preheated oven at 350°F for about 45 minutes, or until a skewer inserted in the thickest part of the cake comes out clean.

Let cool in the pan for 20 minutes, then invert onto a wire rack and let cool completely.

Serve at room temperature dusted with confectioners' sugar, topped with Toffee Topping, or warm with Toffee Sauce or whipped cream.

Store in an airtight container and eat within 5 days.

Plain chocolate and white chocolate in one rich, attractive cake. Serve with chocolate sauce or whipped cream.

double chocolate ripple

2¼ sticks unsalted butter, at room temperature

1¼ cups sugar

4 extra-large eggs, at room temperature

a good pinch of salt

1 teaspoon pure vanilla extract

1¾ cups self-rising flour

3 oz. bittersweet chocolate, chopped

2½ oz. best-quality white chocolate, chopped

1 tablespoon unsweetened cocoa powder

confectioners' sugar, for dusting

a cathedral or other Bundt pan, 9 inches diameter, greased

makes one Bundt cake

Put the butter in an electric mixer and beat until creamy. Increase the speed and gradually beat in the sugar. Lightly beat the eggs, salt, and vanilla in a large measuring cup with a lip, then add to the creamed mixture, about 1 tablespoon at a time, beating well after each addition. Add 1 tablespoon of the flour with the last 2 portions of egg to prevent the mixture from separating.

Sift the rest of the flour onto the mixture and gently fold in with a large metal spoon. Spoon half the mixture into a second bowl.

Put the bittersweet chocolate in a heatproof bowl set over a saucepan of steaming water and melt it gently. Remove the bowl and let cool while you melt the white chocolate in the same way.

Sift the cocoa onto one bowl of cake mixture, add the cooled melted bittersweet chocolate, and mix gently.

Using a clean metal spoon, stir the melted white chocolate into the other bowl of cake mixture.

Spoon both mixtures into the pan, using each mixture alternately. To make the marbling, draw a knife through the mixtures and swirl together.

Bake in a preheated oven at 350°F for about 50 minutes or until a skewer inserted in the thickest part of the cake comes out clean. Let cool for 20 minutes, then invert onto a wire rack and let cool completely. Serve dusted with confectioners' sugar.

Store in an airtight container and eat within 5 days.

Elegant enough to serve for a dinner party with whipped cream or Chocolate Fudge Sauce (page 61)—or make as a batch of muffins to take to work.

hazelnut chocolate mini cakes

1½ cups ready-skinned (white) hazelnuts

6 extra-large egg whites

1 cup all-purpose flour

1 cup unsweetened cocoa powder

1½ cups confectioners' sugar

⅓ cup firmly packed moist light brown sugar

1½ sticks unsalted butter, melted and cooled

a mini Bundt pan or 12-cup muffin pan, lined with paper cases

makes 6 mini Bundt cakes or 12 muffins

Put the nuts in a baking dish and toast in a preheated oven at 300°F until a good even golden brown, about 15 minutes. Cool, then transfer to a processor and pulse to make a fairly fine powder. Increase the oven heat to 400°F.

Put the egg whites in a spotlessly clean, grease-free bowl and beat until soft peaks form. Sift the flour, cocoa, confectioners' sugar and brown sugar onto the egg whites. Add the ground hazelnuts and cooled melted butter and gently fold all the ingredients together with a large metal spoon.

Spoon the cake mixture into the Bundt pan or muffin cups to fill evenly. Bake in the heated oven for 20 minutes until firm to the touch. Let cool in the pan for 5 minutes, then gently invert onto a wire rack and let cool completely.

Store in an airtight container and eat within 3 days.

An old-fashioned coffee cake, made in a cathedral-design Bundt pan, with plenty of crunchy nut streusel inside.

traditional pecan coffee cake

streusel

1 cup finely chopped pecans

¼ cup firmly packed moist dark brown sugar

1½ teaspoons ground cinnamon

batter

2 sticks plus 1 tablespoon unsalted butter, at room temperature

2 extra-large eggs, at room temperature, beaten

¾ cup sugar

1 cup sour cream

2 cups all-purpose flour

½ teaspoon baking soda

2 teaspoons baking powder

a good pinch of salt

confectioners' sugar, for dusting

a cathedral or other Bundt pan, 9 inches diameter, well greased

a rubber spatula

makes one Bundt cake

Make the streusel topping mixture first. Mix the pecans, sugar and cinnamon in small bowl and set aside.

To make the batter, put the butter, eggs, sugar, and sour cream in a large bowl and beat with an electric mixer on medium speed until smooth and well mixed.

Sift the flour, baking soda, baking powder, and salt onto the mixture and mix in gently.

Spoon half the batter into the pan and spread it evenly with a rubber spatula. Sprinkle with half the streusel mixture. Spoon the rest of the batter into the pan and spread evenly. Sprinkle with the remaining streusel, then gently press the mixture onto the surface of the batter with the back of a spoon.

Bake in a preheated oven at 350°F for 45–55 minutes or until a skewer inserted in the thickest part of the cake comes out clean. Remove the pan from the oven and transfer to a wire rack. Let cool completely, then invert onto a serving platter. Dust with confectioners' sugar before serving.

Store in an airtight container and eat within 4 days.

Chef Robert Carmack makes this unusually flavored pound cake for Christmas and New Year parties, replacing the milk with brandy or bourbon.

festive fruit and nut pound cake

2 sticks unsalted butter, at room temperature

1 cup plus 2 tablespoons sugar

4 extra-large eggs, at room temperature

3 tablespoons milk, brandy, or bourbon

½ teaspoon pure vanilla extract

1 cup (3 oz.) mixed raisins and golden raisins

1 cup chopped pecans

1¾ cups self-rising flour

a pinch of salt

¼ teaspoon ground mace

¼ teaspoon freshly grated nutmeg

confectioners' sugar, for dusting

a cathedral or other Bundt pan, 9 inches diameter, well greased

makes one Bundt cake

Put the butter and sugar in a bowl and, using an electric mixer or whisk, beat well until light and fluffy. Break the eggs into a large measuring cup with a lip, add the milk (or brandy or bourbon) and vanilla, and mix with a fork. Gradually add to the butter mixture, about 1 tablespoon at a time, beating well after each addition.

Put the fruit and pecans in a bowl, add 1 tablespoon of the flour, and toss gently.

Sift the remaining flour, salt, mace, and nutmeg onto the creamed mixture and gently fold in with a large metal spoon. Add the reserved flour to the fruit and pecans and toss gently. Add this mixture to the cake mixture and stir gently. Transfer to the prepared pan and spread evenly.

Bake in a preheated oven at 350°F for 45–50 minutes, or until a skewer inserted in the thickest part of the cake comes out clean. Let cool in the pan, then invert onto a wire rack and let cool completely. Serve dusted with confectioners' sugar. Best eaten the next day.

Store in an airtight container and eat within 5 days.

As coffee cakes go, this recipe seems rather plain and simple, but the flavor is superb. Serve for dinner with whipped cream.

whiskey coffee cake
with golden raisins and sour cream

⅓ cup golden raisins

2 tablespoons Irish whiskey or orange juice

1½ sticks unsalted butter, at room temperature

1⅓ cups firmly packed moist light brown sugar

2 tablespoons maple syrup

4 extra-large eggs, at room temperature, beaten

2¾ cups all-purpose flour

½ teaspoon baking soda

2 teaspoons baking powder

a good pinch of salt

½ cup sour cream

glaze

¼ cup Irish whiskey or orange juice

¼ cup maple syrup

a cathedral or other Bundt pan, 9 inches diameter, well greased

a rubber spatula

makes one Bundt cake

Put the raisins and whiskey in a small bowl, stir, and set aside while you make the rest of the batter.

Put the butter, sugar, and maple syrup in a large bowl and beat on high speed with an electric mixer or whisk until light and fluffy. Gradually add the eggs, beating well after each addition.

Sift the flour, baking soda, baking powder, and salt into the bowl. Add the sour cream, soaked raisins, and whiskey and gently mix all the ingredients with a large metal spoon.

Spoon into the prepared pan and spread evenly with a rubber spatula. Bake in a preheated oven at 350°F for 50–60 minutes or until a skewer inserted in the thickest part of the cake comes out clean. Remove the pan from the oven and transfer to a wire rack. Let cool for 20 minutes while you make the glaze.

Put the whiskey and maple syrup in a small saucepan and heat gently. Invert the pan onto a deep plate, lift off the pan, then spoon the glaze over the warm cake. Let cool completely.

Store in an airtight container and eat within 4 days.

An old recipe combining dried dates and walnuts for a well-textured, moist cake.

1½ cups pitted chopped dates

¾ cup boiling water

1¾ sticks unsalted butter, at room temperature

1½ cups firmly packed moist dark brown sugar

3 extra-large eggs, at room temperature, beaten

3 cups all-purpose flour

1½ teaspoons baking soda

2 teaspoons baking powder

1 teaspoon freshly grated nutmeg

½ teaspoon ground cloves or allspice

½ teaspoon ground cinnamon

a good pinch of salt

1 cup sour cream

¾ cup walnut pieces

confectioners' sugar, for dusting

a rubber spatula

a cathedral or other Bundt pan, 9 inches diameter, well greased

makes one Bundt cake

spiced sour cream and date coffee cake

Put the dates and boiling water in a food processor and pulse or process very briefly to make a coarse purée. Let cool while you make the rest of the batter.

Put the butter and sugar in a large bowl and beat with an electric mixer or whisk until very light in color and texture. Gradually add the eggs, beating well after each addition.

Sift the flour, baking soda, baking powder, nutmeg, cloves, cinnamon, and salt into the bowl. Add the sour cream, the cooled date mixture, and walnuts and mix gently with a large metal spoon or rubber spatula.

Spoon into the prepared pan and spread evenly using the spatula.

Bake in a preheated oven at 350°F for 50–60 minutes or until a skewer inserted in the thickest part of the cake comes out clean. Remove from the oven, leave the pan on a wire rack for 20 minutes, then carefully invert onto the rack to cool completely. Dust with confectioners' sugar before serving.

Store in an airtight container and eat within 5 days.

A good cake for breakfast, or for dinner, served with Toffee Sauce (page 61) or whipped cream.

mini gingerbreads

1⅔ cups self-rising flour

1 teaspoon baking soda

1 tablespoon ground ginger

1 teaspoon apple pie spice

¼ teaspoon freshly grated nutmeg

¼ teaspoon ground cloves

1 stick unsalted butter, diced

½ cup molasses

½ cup light corn syrup

⅔ cup firmly packed dark brown sugar

1¼ cups milk

1 extra-large egg, beaten

a mini Bundt pan, greased

makes 6 mini Bundt cakes

Sift the flour, baking soda, ginger, apple pie spice, nutmeg, and cloves onto a sheet of wax paper, then tip into a food processor. Add the diced butter and process until the mixture looks like very fine crumbs.

Put the molasses, corn syrup, sugar, and milk in a pan and heat gently until the sugar dissolves. Cool until lukewarm, then, with the machine running, pour the mixture through the feed tube. Add the egg in the same way and process until just thoroughly mixed.

Spoon the mixture into the prepared mini pan until the cups are equally filled and bake in a preheated oven at 350°F for 20 minutes until firm to the touch. Let cool for 15 minutes before inverting onto a wire rack.

Store in an airtight container and eat within 5 days.

This is a cake with plenty of flavor, but not too sweet or rich. The creamy topping can be served separately.

well-spiced carrot cake

1¾ cups self-rising flour

1 teaspoon baking powder

2 teaspoons ground cinnamon

1 teaspoon ground ginger

½ teaspoon freshly grated nutmeg

⅔ cup firmly packed moist light brown sugar

¾ cup safflower oil

3 extra-large eggs

3½ cups grated carrots, about 5 medium

½ cup walnut or pecan pieces, plus extra to decorate

mascarpone lemon cream

1 cup (8 oz.) mascarpone cheese

½ cup confectioners' sugar, sifted

1 tablespoon lemon juice

a cathedral or other Bundt pan, 9 inches diameter, well greased

makes one Bundt cake

Sift the flour, baking powder, cinnamon, ginger, nutmeg, and sugar into a large bowl. Make a hollow in the center.

Put the oil and eggs in a large measuring cup with a lip, beat well, then pour into the hollow in the dry ingredients. Mix well with a wooden spoon, then stir in the grated carrots and nuts.

Transfer the mixture to the prepared pan and spread evenly. Bake in a preheated oven at 350°F for 45–55 minutes or until a skewer inserted in the thickest part of the cake comes out clean. Let cool for 15 minutes, then invert onto a wire rack and let cool completely.

To make the topping, mix the mascarpone with the confectioners' sugar, then stir in the lemon juice.

Decorate the top of the cake with some of the topping, then add the nuts. Serve the rest of the mascarpone lemon cream separately.

Store in an airtight container in a very cool place or the refrigerator and eat within 4 days.

For the best texture, use fine cornmeal or regular polenta rather than the instant variety. A mild, fruity oil will give the best flavor.

italian lemon pistachio miniature cakes

2 extra-large eggs, at room temperature

⅔ cup sugar

freshly grated zest of 1 large unwaxed lemon

¾ cup milk (or half each of milk and Marsala)

¾ cup virgin olive oil

1 cup all-purpose flour

2 tablespoons fine cornmeal or polenta

1 tablespoon baking powder

a pinch of salt

⅓ cup coarsely chopped pistachio nuts

confectioners' sugar, for dusting

a mini Bundt pan, greased, or a 12-cup muffin pan, lined with paper cases

makes 6 mini Bundt cakes or 12 muffins

Put the eggs and sugar in a large bowl and, using an electric mixer or whisk, beat until very thick and pale. On low speed, beat in the lemon zest, followed by the milk (or milk and Marsala) and olive oil.

Sift the flour, polenta, baking powder, and salt onto the mixture and gently fold into the batter with a large metal spoon. When there are no more streaks of flour to be seen, mix in the nuts, then transfer to the prepared pan. Spread evenly, then bake in a preheated oven at 400°F for about 20 minutes or until springy when pressed.

Let cool in the pan for 5 minutes, then invert onto a wire rack and let cool completely. Dust with confectioners' sugar before serving with coffee, or fresh fruit and whipped cream, or mascarpone lemon cream (page 35).

Store in an airtight container and eat within 2 days.

This cake made with fresh (or defrosted) cranberries has been a Thanksgiving favorite since I first tasted it at a New England Cranberry Festival.

thanksgiving cranberry bundt

filling

½ cup whole blanched almonds

2 cups fresh cranberries

2 teaspoons ground cinnamon

½ cup firmly packed moist light brown sugar

batter

1 stick unsalted butter, at room temperature

2 extra-large eggs, at room temperature, beaten

1 cup firmly packed moist light brown sugar

1 cup sour cream

3 tablespoons finely chopped almonds

2 cups all-purpose flour

1 teaspoon ground cinnamon

½ teaspoon baking soda

1 teaspoon baking powder

confectioners' sugar for dusting

a cathedral or other Bundt pan, 9 inches diameter, well greased

makes one Bundt cake

Make the filling first. Put the almonds in a food processor and chop finely to make a very coarse powder. Transfer to a large bowl.

Put the cranberries in the processor and chop coarsely. Add to the almonds, then add the cinnamon and sugar and mix well. Set aside.

To make the batter, put the butter, beaten eggs, sugar, sour cream, and chopped almonds in another bowl. Beat with an electric mixer or whisk on medium speed until very smooth. Sift the flour, cinnamon, baking soda, and baking powder onto the mixture, then stir in with a large metal spoon. When thoroughly blended, spoon half the batter into the prepared pan. Sprinkle the cranberry mixture over the top, then add the rest of the batter.

Bake in a preheated oven at 350°F for about 50 minutes or until a skewer inserted in the thickest part of the cake comes out clean. Let cool in the pan for 15 minutes, then carefully invert onto a wire rack, dust with confectioners' sugar, and let cool completely. Store in an airtight container and eat within 4 days.

Blueberry Variation In summer, use fresh blueberries for a fresh fruit Bundt. Make the batter as in the main recipe, but omit the cinnamon and add the grated zest of ½ unwaxed lemon.

To make the filling, mix 1½ cups fresh blueberries with ½ cup light brown sugar, ½ cup chopped almonds, and the grated zest of ½ unwaxed lemon. Proceed as in the main recipe.

daisy cakes

This may seem a strange way to make a cake, but the final result is rich and moist, rather like a brownie.

processor mocha fudge cake

¾ cup all-purpose flour

1 teaspoon baking powder

½ teaspoon baking soda

a pinch of salt

2 oz. bittersweet chocolate

2 tablespoons unsweetened cocoa powder

1 cup sugar

⅓ cup very hot water

2 extra-large eggs, at room temperature, beaten

1½ sticks unsalted butter, at room temperature, diced

2 tablespoons espresso coffee or dark rum

½ cup sour cream

glaze

3 oz. bittersweet chocolate, broken up

2 tablespoons unsalted butter

¼ cup confectioners' sugar, sifted

3 tablespoons espresso coffee (or 2 tablespoons water and 1 tablespoon dark rum)

a daisy cake pan, 11 x 8½ x 2 inches, greased

makes one daisy cake

Sift the flour, baking powder, baking soda, and salt onto a sheet of wax paper.

Break up the chocolate and put in a food processor. Add the cocoa and half the sugar. Run the machine until the ingredients form a coarse powder, then, with the machine still running, pour in the hot water through the feed tube.

As soon as the chocolate has melted, pour in the beaten eggs, followed by rest of the sugar. After 30 seconds, stop the machine and scrape down the bowl. Add the butter, process for 1 minute, then stop the machine and scrape down the bowl again. Add the coffee and sour cream and process for a few seconds, until just mixed. Add the flour mixture and process a few seconds more to make a smooth, even batter.

Pour the mixture into the prepared pan, spread it right into the corners, then bake in a preheated oven at 325°F for 45–50 minutes, until a skewer inserted in the center comes out clean. Let cool in the pan, then invert onto a serving platter.

To make the glaze, put the chocolate, butter, confectioners' sugar, and coffee (or water and rum) in a small saucepan. Set over the lowest possible heat and stir gently until melted and smooth. Remove from the heat. Leave until thick enough to coat the cake, then pour or spoon over the cake and leave until set.

Store in an airtight container. Best eaten within 4 days.

A truly rich and moist cake made without flour, but with plenty of chocolate.

fudgy pecan cake

12 oz. bittersweet chocolate

1½ sticks unsalted butter

½ cup unsweetened cocoa powder, sifted

5 extra-large eggs, at room temperature

1¼ cups sugar

1 cup pecan pieces, coarsely chopped

confectioners' sugar, for dusting

a daisy cake pan, 11 x 8½ x 2 inches, greased

makes one daisy cake

Break up the chocolate and put in a heatproof bowl with the butter. Set the bowl over a saucepan of steaming hot water and melt gently, stirring frequently. Remove the bowl from the pan and stir in the cocoa.

Put the eggs in a large electric mixer and beat well. Add the sugar and beat on high speed until the mixture is very light and fluffy and has tripled in volume. Remove the bowl from the mixer.

Using a large metal spoon, carefully fold in the chocolate mixture followed by the pecans.

Spoon into the prepared pan and spread evenly. Bake in a preheated oven at 350°F for about 30 minutes until the top of the cake is firm, but the center still slightly soft. Let cool for 10 minutes, then invert onto a wire rack. Dust with confectioners' sugar and serve at room temperature or warm with whipped cream.

Store in an airtight container and eat within 4 days.

This cake is a simple, all-in-one mixture spiked with fresh orange zest and juice and covered with glaze richly flavored with fresh orange juice or orange liqueur.

fresh orange cake with sticky glaze

2 sticks unsalted butter, very soft

1¼ cups sugar

4 extra-large eggs

2¼ cups self-rising flour

1 teaspoon baking powder

a pinch of salt

the grated zest and juice of
1 large unwaxed orange

glaze

1 stick unsalted butter

⅓ cup sugar

⅓ cup fresh orange juice,
orange liqueur or whiskey

*a daisy cake pan,
11 x 8½ x 2 inches, greased*

makes one daisy cake

To make the cake, put the butter and sugar in a large bowl, then add the eggs, flour, baking powder, salt, and orange zest and juice. Beat with a wooden spoon or electric whisk or mixer on low speed for 1 minute until smooth and thoroughly blended.

Spoon the mixture into the prepared pan and smooth the surface. Bake in a preheated oven at 350°F for 40–45 minutes or until a skewer inserted in the center comes out clean.

Towards the end of the baking time, prepare the glaze. Put the butter, sugar, and orange juice in a small saucepan and heat gently until melted. Keep the mixture warm.

When the cake is cooked, lift it out of the oven, but keep it in the pan for 5 minutes. Invert onto a serving platter with a slight rim. Prick the cake all over with a skewer. Reheat the glaze, if necessary, and spoon it evenly over the cake. Let cool. Serve at room temperature with whipped cream.

Store in an airtight container and eat within 4 days.

One of the easiest, quickest, and prettiest cakes you can make. The all-in-one lemon cake can be made from scratch in under an hour—the simple fruit topping takes just a couple of minutes to arrange.

citrus summer cake

1½ sticks unsalted butter, softened but not oily

1¼ cups sugar

3 extra-large eggs, at room temperature, beaten

1¾ cups self-rising flour

½ teaspoon baking powder

½ cup milk

grated zest of 2 medium unwaxed lemons

topping

¼ cup Lemon Curd (page 62)

2 tablespoons toasted slivered almonds

2 cups (8 oz.) mixed berries (such as strawberries, raspberries, blueberries, and blackberries)

confectioners' sugar, for dusting

a daisy cake pan, 11 x 8½ x 2 inches, greased

makes one daisy cake

To make the cake, put the butter, sugar, eggs, flour, baking powder, milk, and lemon zest in an electric mixer. On medium speed, beat until the mixture is thick and fluffy with no sign of lumps or streaks of flour.

Spoon into the prepared pan and spread evenly. Bake in a preheated oven at 350°F for about 30 minutes, or until a skewer inserted in the center comes out clean. Let cool in the pan for 10 minutes, then invert onto a wire rack and let cool completely. When cold, the cake can be stored in an airtight container for up to 2 days.

When ready to serve, set the cake on a serving platter. Brush the sides and top of the cake with the Lemon Curd, then sprinkle slivered almonds all over it. Arrange the berries on top and around the cake, dust with confectioners' sugar, and serve.

Store in an airtight container in the refrigerator and eat within 2 days.

This traditional cake, made with equal weights of butter, sugar, eggs, and flour, needs plenty of beating to add air and lightness. Here the work is done with an electric mixer, and the dried berries add a burst of flavor.

blueberry lemon pound cake

2¼ sticks unsalted butter, at room temperature

1¼ cups sugar

grated zest of 1 large unwaxed lemon

4 extra-large eggs, at room temperature

a pinch of salt

1¾ cups self-rising flour

1 cup freeze-dried blueberries or ½ cup soft dried blueberries

confectioners' sugar, for dusting

a daisy cake pan, 11 x 8½ x 2 inches, greased

makes one daisy cake

Put the butter in an electric mixer and beat at low speed until creamy. Increase the speed and gradually beat in the sugar, followed by the lemon zest.

Put the eggs and salt in a large measuring cup with a lip, beat lightly, then add to the creamed mixture, 1 tablespoon or so at a time, beating well after each addition. Add 1 tablespoon flour with the last 2 portions of egg to prevent the mixture from separating.

Sift the rest of the flour onto the mixture and gently fold in with a large metal spoon. When you no longer see streaks of flour, mix in the blueberries.

Transfer to the prepared pan and spread evenly. Bake in a preheated oven at 350°F for about 40 minutes or until a skewer inserted in the center comes out clean. Let cool in the pan for 10 minutes, then carefully invert onto a wire rack and let cool completely. Dust with confectioners' sugar before serving.

Store in an airtight container and eat within 5 days.

Use tart apples for the best flavor—varieties such as Granny Smith, Newtown Pippin, or Northern Spy.

apple and walnut honey spice cake

1 cup honey

1 stick unsalted butter, softened

⅔ cup firmly packed moist light brown sugar

2 extra-large eggs, beaten

2 cups self-rising flour

2 teaspoons apple pie spice

4 medium apples, peeled, cored, and chopped (3 cups chopped)

1 cup walnut pieces

confectioners' sugar, for dusting

a daisy cake pan, 11 x 8½ x 2 inches, greased

makes one daisy cake

Put the honey, butter, sugar, and eggs in a large bowl. Sift the flour and apple pie spice into the bowl, then stir gently with a wooden spoon or use an electric mixer on low speed. When thoroughly mixed, stir in the apples and walnuts. Transfer to the prepared pan and spread evenly.

Bake in a preheated oven at 350°F for 40–50 minutes, until a skewer inserted in the center of the cake comes out clean. Let cool in the pan for 15 minutes, then invert onto a wire rack to cool completely.

Dust with confectioners' sugar, then serve warm or at room temperature with whipped cream on the side.

Store in an airtight container and eat within 3 days.

other cakes

A wonderful, rich combination of roasted hazelnuts, light brown sugar, and thick, dark, chocolate cream.

hazelnut meringue cake

1½ cups ready-skinned (white) hazelnuts

1½ cups firmly packed moist light brown sugar

6 extra-large egg whites

a pinch of salt

chocolate cream

10 oz. good bittersweet chocolate

1⅔ cups heavy cream

unsweetened cocoa powder, grated chocolate, or Chocolate Brittle (page 61), for decorating

2 baking sheets, lined with nonstick baking parchment

makes one 2-layer cake

Put the nuts in a baking dish and toast in a preheated oven at 300°F until they are evenly golden brown, about 10 minutes. Cool, then transfer to a food processor and pulse to make a coarse powder. Reserve 2 tablespoons of the sugar and add the remainder to the food processor. Pulse to mix and set aside.

Put the egg whites and salt in a spotlessly clean, grease-free bowl and beat with an electric mixer or whisk until soft peaks form. Beat in the reserved 2 tablespoons sugar, beating until the meringue is stiff and glossy. Using a large metal spoon, very gently fold in the nut and sugar mixture.

Divide the mixture in half, and spoon 1 portion into the center of each prepared sheet. Spread out each portion to a circle about 8 inches across. Bake in the preheated oven at 300°F for 1¼–1½ hours until golden, firm, and crisp. If necessary, rotate the sheets so the meringues cook evenly. Let cool completely, then peel off the paper.

Meanwhile, to make the chocolate cream, break up the chocolate into small squares and put in a food processor. Gently heat the cream until scalding hot but not boiling. With the machine running, pour the cream through the feed tube into the bowl of chocolate. As soon as the mixture has become smooth and thick, turn off the machine. In warm weather, chill until thick enough to spread.

Put a circle of meringue on a serving platter and spread with about one-third of the chocolate cream. Top with the second circle, then quickly cover the top and sides with the rest of the chocolate cream. Chill until ready to serve, then sprinkle with cocoa, grated chocolate, or Chocolate Brittle.

The cake can be kept in an airtight container in the refrigerator for up to 3 days.

The best shortcake is somewhere between a biscuit, shortbread, and cake, with a crunchy crust and soft, rich, tender crumb. Try blueberries, blackberries, or raspberries instead of strawberries, and lemon instead of orange.

strawberry shortcake

4 cups (1 lb.) ripe strawberries, hulled

1–2 tablespoons sugar, to taste

2 tablespoons fresh orange juice or orange liqueur

shortcake

1¾ cups self-rising flour, plus extra for working

a large pinch of salt

½ teaspoon baking powder

the grated zest 1 unwaxed orange

½ cup sugar, plus extra for sprinkling

5½ tablespoons unsalted butter, chilled and diced

about 1 cup heavy cream, chilled

2 tablespoons unsalted butter, softened, for brushing

a large bowl whipped cream, for serving

a 3-inch biscuit cutter

a baking sheet, greased

makes 6

Thickly slice the strawberries into a bowl. Sprinkle with the sugar and juice, then mix gently. Cover and leave at room temperature.

Put the flour, salt, baking powder, orange zest, and sugar in a food processor and blend for 5 seconds until just mixed. Add the butter and process until the mixture looks like bread crumbs. With the machine running, pour the cream through the feed tube and mix until the dough comes together to form a soft but not sticky ball.

Carefully remove the dough from the processor and put on a lightly floured work surface. Flour your hands and pat out the dough until it is a good 1 inch thick. Cut out rounds using the cookie cutter, gently kneading the trimmings and patting them out again, to give 6 rounds in all.

Set the rounds slightly apart on the prepared sheet and sprinkle the tops with a little sugar. Bake in a preheated oven at 425°F for 10 minutes. Reduce to 350°F and cook for a further 10 minutes until the shortcakes are firm and golden.

Remove the sheet from the oven and brush the tops of the cakes with very soft butter. Let cool on the sheet. When firm and completely cooled, split the cakes in half horizontally, but leave in pairs.

When ready to serve, gently warm the shortcakes for 5 minutes in a preheated oven at 350°F. Transfer to a serving platter and fill the shortcakes with the whipped cream, berries, and juice. Replace the "lids" and put a few extra slices of berries on top. Serve immediately with extra whipped cream. Best eaten the same day.

A pure white cake made with a dozen egg whites. The easiest way to separate whites from yolks is to use eggs straight from the refrigerator, but for best results leave the whites at room temperature for 30 minutes before beating.

angel's cloud

1 cup cake flour

a pinch of salt

1¼ cups sugar

12 extra-large egg whites

1 teaspoon cream of tartar

the finely grated zest of 1 unwaxed lemon

topping

1 cup heavy cream, chilled

¼ cup Lemon Curd (page 62)

3 cups (1 lb.) blueberries or strawberries

a rubber spatula

a round angel food pan or tube pan, 9¾ x 4 inches deep, ungreased

makes one angel cake

Sift the flour, salt, and one-quarter of the sugar 3 times into a bowl.

Put the egg whites into a spotlessly clean, grease-free bowl and beat with an electric mixer or whisk on medium speed until fluffy. Add the cream of tartar and lemon zest, then beat on high speed just until stiff peaks start to form. Beat in the remaining sugar, 1 tablespoon at a time. Using a large metal spoon or rubber spatula, gently fold in the sifted flour mixture in 3 batches.

Spoon the mixture into the pan and spread evenly with a rubber spatula. Gently tap the pan on the work surface to dislodge any large air pockets. Bake in a preheated oven* at 325°F for about 45 minutes until golden and the cake springs back when gently pressed. Let set and cool completely in the pan—the best way to do this is to invert the pan onto the neck of a funnel or bottle. With a nonstick pan, invert the pan onto a raised wire rack and let cool before gently twisting and lifting off the pan.

Meanwhile to make the topping, whip the cream until soft peaks form, then gently stir in the Lemon Curd.

Carefully unmold the cake and set on a serving platter. Cover with the lemon cream mixture and decorate with berries. Serve immediately or store in an airtight container in the refrigerator and eat within 24 hours. Use a serrated bread knife for cutting.

*Manufacturers of some angel food pans recommend a lower temperature or reduced cooking time—refer to manufacturer's guidelines before use. For this cake, it is important to use an ungreased pan—the idea is to get the brown crust to stick to the pan after baking, leaving a white cake. This will not happen with a nonstick pan.

A traditional yet simple cake from France, flavored with ground almonds. Serve with tea or coffee, or for dessert with fruit salad, cherries, or berries and cream.

french almond cake

1 stick unsalted butter, softened

¾ cup sugar

3 extra-large eggs, beaten

1 cup slivered almonds, ground in a food processor, plus 1 tablespoon extra, for sprinkling

⅓ cup self-rising flour

1 tablespoon milk or kirsch

confectioners' sugar, for dusting

a cake pan, 8 inches diameter, greased and bottom lined with parchment paper

makes one cake

Put the butter, sugar, and eggs in a large bowl, add the ground almonds, flour, and milk, then beat with an electric mixer or whisk. When quite light and fluffy, spoon into the prepared pan and spread evenly. Sprinkle the slivered almonds over the top.

Bake in a preheated oven at 350°F for 30–35 minutes or until the cake just springs back when pressed. Run a round-bladed knife around the inside edge of the pan to loosen the cake, then turn out onto a wire rack and let cool. Dust with confectioners' sugar before serving.

Store in an airtight container and eat within 5 days.

toppings
and sauces

toffee topping

¾ cup firmly packed
moist light brown sugar

1 stick unsalted butter

¼ cup heavy cream

½ teaspoon pure vanilla extract

Put the sugar, butter, and cream in
a small saucepan and heat gently
until melted. Bring to a boil, then
simmer for 3 minutes until thick
and toffee-like. Pour into a
heatproof bowl and let cool. Stir in
the vanilla. Store, tightly covered
in the refrigerator, for up to 1 week.

toffee sauce

Make the topping above, adding
an extra ¼ cup cream. Serve warm.

chocolate fudge sauce

6 oz. bittersweet chocolate, chopped

3 tablespoons unsalted butter

2 tablespoons sugar

2 tablespoons light corn syrup

¾ cup half-and-half

Put all the ingredients in a small,
heavy saucepan and set over low
heat. Stir gently until melted and
smooth. Continue heating and
stirring until the mixture is almost
at boiling point. Remove from the
heat and serve. This sauce can
be stored, tightly covered in the
refrigerator, for up to 4 days.

white chocolate sauce

7 oz. best-quality white chocolate,
chopped

⅓ cup milk

1 cup heavy cream

Gently melt the chocolate in a
heatproof bowl set over a
saucepan of steaming water.
Remove the bowl from the heat
and stir gently until smooth. Gently
heat the milk and cream until
almost boiling, then gently pour
onto the chocolate in a thin stream,
whisking constantly to make a
smooth sauce. Serve immediately.

maple pecan sauce

2 small sweet apples

⅔ cup maple syrup

½ cup pecan halves

Wash the apples and peel only
if the skin is very tough and
tasteless. Quarter and core the
apples and chop into small dice.
Put in a medium saucepan with the
maple syrup and nuts and heat
gently. Serve immediately.

chocolate brittle

An easy decoration—melt good-
quality bittersweet chocolate and
pour onto a baking sheet lined with
nonstick parchment paper. Spread
thinly. The chocolate can be left
plain or sprinkled with sliced nuts.
Leave to set in a cool place then
break up and use to decorate cakes.

crème chantilly

French sweet whipped cream.

1 cup heavy cream

½ teaspoon pure vanilla extract

1½ tablespoons sugar

If possible, chill the bowl and the
whisk in the refrigerator or freezer
for 30 minutes. Pour the cream
into the chilled bowl and whip until
it starts to thicken. Add the vanilla
and sugar and whip again until soft
peaks form—take care not to
overwhip the cream, or it will
separate.

cinnamon cream

Omit the vanilla and add ½ teaspoon
ground cinnamon with the sugar.

maple cream

Omit the vanilla and replace the sugar
with 1½ teaspoons maple sugar.

fresh raspberry preserve

The cheat's recipe for a vibrant, soft-set jam. Because the fruit is not cooked, choose dry, almost-ripe berries and sugar-with-pectin (the type sold for jam and jelly making), and store this preserve in the refrigerator or freezer. Use as a filling, topping, or sauce for plain cakes.

1 cup plus 2 tablespoons sugar-with-pectin or sugar

3 cups (1 lb.) raspberries or strawberries, at room temperature

2 tablespoons freshly squeezed lemon juice

makes about 1½ lb.

Put the sugar in a heatproof bowl (non-aluminum) and warm in a low oven 300°F for 10 minutes. Meanwhile, crush the fruit with a potato masher or fork. Mix the fruit into the warm sugar and stir very well. Leave the bowl in a warm, sunny spot for 1 hour, stirring occasionally to dissolve the sugar. Stir in the lemon juice, then spoon the mixture into freezerproof containers. Cover and leave in a cool spot overnight.

Next day, gently stir the preserve. Chill in the refrigerator for 1–2 days until thickened, then use immediately or freeze for up to 6 months. Defrost in the refrigerator and use immediately.

lemon curd

1 stick unsalted butter

1 cup plus 2 tablespoons sugar

the grated zest and juice of 2 large or 3 medium unwaxed lemons

3 large eggs, beaten

makes about 1 lb.

Put the butter, sugar, and lemon zest and juice in the top of a non-aluminum double boiler or in a saucepan set in a roasting pan of boiling water. Set the double boiler or pan over medium heat, so the water boils gently. Cook the butter mixture, stirring constantly with a wooden spoon, until smooth and melted. Add the eggs and stir until the mixture becomes very thick and opaque—avoid short cuts, because if the mixture boils, the eggs will scramble. Spoon into clean jars. When completely cold, use or cover and store in the refrigerator for up to 2 weeks.

mango sauce

12 oz. bag of frozen mango pieces

freshly squeezed juice of ½ lime

sugar, to taste (optional)

Put the mangoes in a blender or processor with the lime juice. Purée until very smooth. Taste, then add another squeeze of lime or a spoonful of sugar as necessary. Serve immediately or cover tightly and store in the refrigerator for up to 2 days. Use with daisy cakes or mini Bundts.

melba sauce

3 cups (1 lb.) raspberries, fresh or frozen and thawed

confectioners' sugar, to taste

Purée the fruit in a processor or blender. Add the sugar to taste (this will depend on the tartness of the fruit and your own preference). Process for 1 minute more to make sure the sugar has dissolved. The sauce can be served as it is, or strained to remove the seeds. Serve immediately or cover and store in the refrigerator for up to 2 days. Use with daisy cakes or mini Bundts.

index

angel's cloud, 57
apple and walnut honey spice cake, 50

banana fudge layer cake, 14
blueberry lemon pound cake, 49
Bundt cakes, 18–39

carrot cake, well-spiced, 35
chocolate:
    chocolate brittle, 61
    chocolate fudge sauce, 61
    chocolate spice cake, 19
    double chocolate ripple, 20
    fudgy pecan cake, 42
    processor mocha fudge cake, 41
    triple chocolate layer cake, 9
    white chocolate sauce, 61
cinnamon cream, 61
citrus summer cake, 46
crème chantilly, 61

daisy cakes, 40–51
double chocolate ripple, 20

festive fruit and nut pound cake, 27
French almond cake, 58
fresh orange cake with sticky glaze, 45
fresh pineapple layer cake, 13
fresh raspberry preserve, 62
fruit:
    apple and walnut honey spice cake, 50
    banana fudge layer cake, 14
    blueberry lemon pound cake, 49
    citrus summer cake, 46
    fresh orange cake with sticky glaze, 45
    fresh pineapple layer cake, 13
    fresh raspberry preserve, 62
    Italian lemon pistachio miniature cakes, 36
    lemon curd, 62
    mango sauce, 63
    Melba sauce, 63
    raspberries-and-cream layer cake, 17

spiced date sour cream coffee cake, 31
strawberry shortcakes, 54
Thanksgiving cranberry Bundt, 39
fudgy pecan cake, 42

gingerbreads, mini, 32

hazelnut meringue cake, 53

Italian lemon pistachio miniature cakes, 36

layer cakes, 8–17
lemon curd, 62

mango sauce, 63
maple:
    cream, 61
    pecan sauce, 61
    syrup pecan cake, 10
Melba sauce, 63

pound cake, festive fruit and nut, 27
processor mocha fudge cake, 41

raspberries-and-cream layer cake, 17

sauces:
    chocolate fudge sauce, 61
    maple pecan sauce, 61
    Melba sauce, 63
    toffee sauce, 61
toffee topping, 61
white chocolate sauce, 61
spiced date sour cream coffee cake, 31
strawberry shortcakes, 54

Thanksgiving cranberry Bundt, 39
toffee sauce, 61
toffee topping, 61
toppings and sauces, 60–63
traditional pecan coffee cake, 24
triple chocolate layer cake, 9

well-spiced carrot cake, 35
whiskey coffee cake, 28

conversion chart

Weights and measures have been rounded up or down slightly to make measuring easier.

Volume equivalents:

American	Metric	Imperial
1 teaspoon	5 ml	
1 tablespoon	15 ml	
¼ cup	60 ml	2 fl.oz.
⅓ cup	75 ml	2½ fl.oz.
½ cup	125 ml	4 fl.oz.
⅔ cup	150 ml	5 fl.oz. (¼ pint)
¾ cup	175 ml	6 fl.oz.
1 cup	250 ml	8 fl.oz.

Weight equivalents: **Measurements:**

Imperial	Metric	Inches	Cm
1 oz.	25 g	¼ inch	5 mm
2 oz.	50 g	½ inch	1 cm
3 oz.	75 g	¾ inch	1.5 cm
4 oz.	125 g	1 inch	2.5 cm
5 oz.	150 g	2 inches	5 cm
6 oz.	175 g	3 inches	7 cm
7 oz.	200 g	4 inches	10 cm
8 oz. (½ lb.)	250 g	5 inches	12 cm
9 oz.	275 g	6 inches	15 cm
10 oz.	300 g	7 inches	18 cm
11 oz.	325 g	8 inches	20 cm
12 oz.	375 g	9 inches	23 cm
13 oz.	400 g	10 inches	25 cm
14 oz.	425 g	11 inches	28 cm
15 oz.	475 g	12 inches	30 cm
16 oz. (1 lb.)	500 g		
2 lb.	1 kg		

Oven temperatures:

110°C	(225°F)	Gas ¼
120°C	(250°F)	Gas ½
140°C	(275°F)	Gas 1
150°C	(300°F)	Gas 2
160°C	(325°F)	Gas 3
180°C	(350°F)	Gas 4
190°C	(375°F)	Gas 5
200°C	(400°F)	Gas 6
220°C	(425°F)	Gas 7
230°C	(450°F)	Gas 8
240°C	(475°F)	Gas 9